SPEED RACERS

By
Kirsty Holmes

CRABTREE
PUBLISHING COMPANY
WWW.CRABTREEBOOKS.COM

CRABTREE
PUBLISHING COMPANY
WWW.CRABTREEBOOKS.COM

**Published
in Canada
Crabtree Publishing**
616 Welland Avenue
St. Catharines, ON
L2M 5V6

**Published in
the United States
Crabtree Publishing**
PMB 59051
350 Fifth Ave, 59th Floor
New York, NY 10118

Published in 2019 by Crabtree Publishing Company

Author: Kirsty Holmes

Editors: Holly Duhig, Petrice Custance

Design: Gareth Liddington

Proofreader: Melissa Boyce

**Production coordinator and
prepress technician:** Margaret Amy Salter

Print coordinator: Katherine Berti

All facts, statistics, web addresses and URLs in this book were verified as valid and accurate at time of writing. No responsibility for any changes to external websites or references can be accepted by either the author or publisher.

Printed in the U.S.A./012019/CG20181123

Photo credits:
Cover – , 2 – Swill Klitch, 4 – Swill Klitch, 5 – Giuseppe_R, Saikorn, Niphon Subsri, 10 – Blan–k, A–spring, Prostock–studio, adamziaja.com, 11 – GooGag, IconBunny, 18 – VitalityVill, 22 – pluie_r, 23 – Evan-Amos, Boffy b.

Images are courtesy of Shutterstock.com. With thanks to Getty Images, Thinkstock Photo and iStockphoto.

Imagery courtesy of Codemasters. Codemasters, EGO and the Codemasters logo are registered trade marks owned by Codemasters. With thanks to Slightly Mad Studios, Project CARS2, Aston Martin, Jaguar and Porsche Forza Motorsport images courtesy of Microsoft and Turn 10 studios. All rights reserved. With thanks to Amy Ellison. WipEout images courtesy of Sony Interactive Entertainment, all rights reserved. With thanks.

Library and Archives Canada Cataloguing in Publication

Holmes, Kirsty, author
    Speed racers / Kirsty Holmes.

(Game on!)
Includes index.
Issued in print and electronic formats.
ISBN 978-0-7787-5261-5 (hardcover).--
ISBN 978-0-7787-5329-2 (softcover).--
ISBN 978-1-4271-2190-5 (HTML)

    1. Simulation games--Juvenile literature. 2. Video games--Juvenile literature. 3. Electronic games--Juvenile literature. I. Title.

GV1469.15.H647 2018   j794.8'672   C2018-906133-2
                                                 C2018-906134-0

Library of Congress Cataloging-in-Publication Data

Names: Holmes, Kirsty, author.
Title: Speed racers / Kirsty Holmes.
Description: New York, New York : Crabtree Publishing, 2019. |
    Includes index.
Identifiers: LCCN 2018053428 (print) | LCCN 2018057704 (ebook) |
    ISBN 9781427121905 (Electronic) |
    ISBN 9780778752615 (hardcover : alk. paper) |
    ISBN 9780778753292 (pbk. : alk. paper)
Subjects: LCSH: Automobile racing--Computer games--Juvenile literature. |
    Video games--Juvenile literature.
Classification: LCC GV1469.3 (ebook) | LCC GV1469.3 .H679 2019 (print) |
    DDC 794.8--dc23
LC record available at https://lccn.loc.gov/2018053428

CONTENTS

WELCOME TO THE ARCADE

Do you love to rush home from school, leap into the driver's seat, and zoom around the tracks? In order to become an amazing racing gamer you need impressive driving skills and quick **reflexes**, and you can't be afraid of a crash or two! This gaming guide will help you improve your racing skills and leave others eating your dust. So what are we waiting for? Let's get your game on!

Hey, speed racer! I'm going to practice my racing skills here in the Arcade for a while before I hit the racetrack. Want to join me?

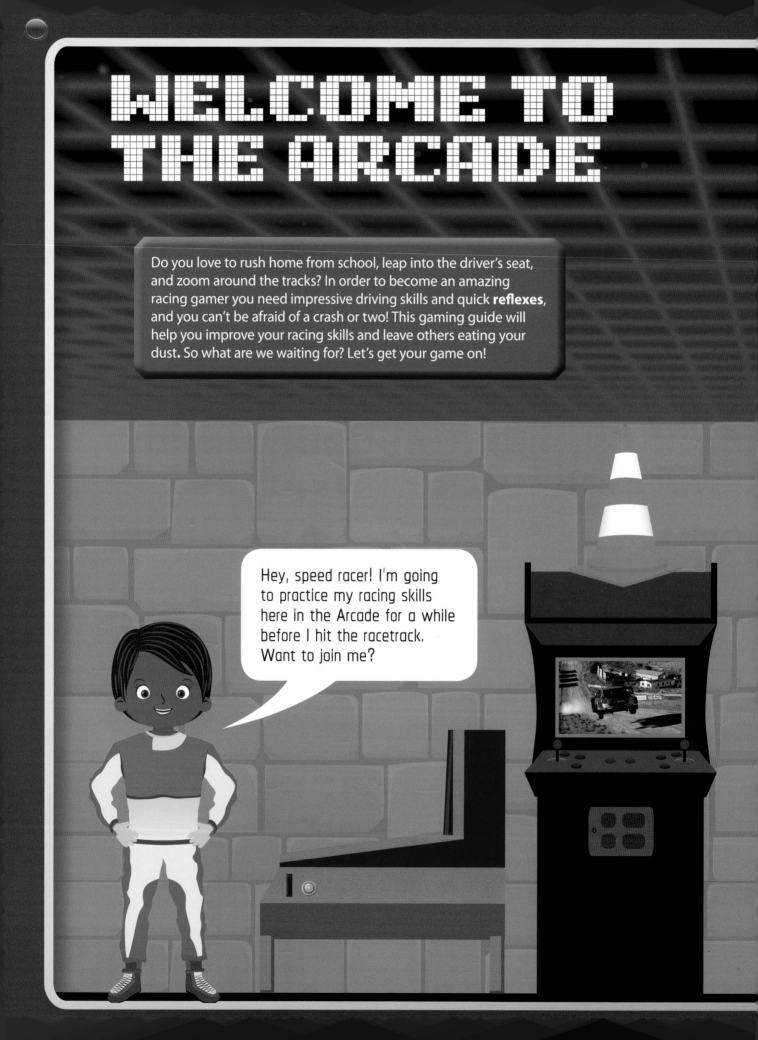

To begin with, a video game is an **electronic** game. A player uses a device to make stuff happen on a screen. That screen can be on a television or personal computer (PC), but you can also play games on smartphones, handheld gaming devices, and tablets. You will need a **console** to play on your television screen. There are many types of video games, such as action-adventure, puzzle, racing, and building games. No matter what your interests are, there is a video game for you!

On your marks... get set...
INTO THE ARCADE!

<<Player One... Ready...?>>

ARCADE

DATA FILE: RACING GAMES

<<LOADING... DATA LEVEL ONE:
WHAT IS A RACING GAME?>>

Racing games are competitive games where players control a vehicle, such as a car, motorbike, or even a spaceship, and take part in a race. The race can either be against opponents, or other players, against the player's own best performance, or against the computer. The aim is to win the race. There are various levels of difficulty. In some games, players only need to steer. In more complicated games, players use pedals and controls just like in a real car. Racing games can be played at home on a PC or console, or in public arcades where games can include real motorbikes or realistic car seats.

CIRCUIT

START/FINISH

TRACK

OPPONENT

PLAYER
VEHICLE

RACING SIMULATOR

Simulator games have very realistic **graphics**. They try to give the player the feeling that they are really driving. These games are often used by professional racing drivers for practice!

ACTION-ARCADE RACING GAMES

These games are less realistic, featuring fantasy worlds or giving the cars powers that they wouldn't have in real life. For example, games such as Mario Kart have speed boosts, bombs, and flying cars!

KART RACER

These games are similar to cartoons. They often feature popular characters and crazy tracks. Sometimes the characters have weapons or traps.

FIRST-PERSON RACER

In first-person racers, the player views the game from inside the car, as if really driving.

THIRD-PERSON RACER

In third-person racers, the player views the action of the game from outside the vehicle.

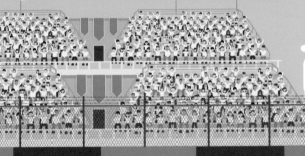

POS: 3RD ← POSITION INDICATOR

LAP: 7/10 ← LAPS TO GO

TIME: 0:32:49 ← LAP TIME

FACT FILE: WipEout

At one time, video games mostly just had cute little heroes such as Mario the plumber running here, there, and everywhere. That began to change around 1995, when Sony introduced the first PlayStation. One of the console's first games was called WipEout. It included **3-D** graphics, which were new at the time. The new graphics helped make video games look more like movies.

WipEout is a super-fast racing game where players take control of floating cars that zoom around the racing tracks of the future. When it was released, the game moved faster than pretty much any game that had come before it. Players loved the challenge of hitting power boosts and sliding around corners as carefully as possible.

It might have been the fastest game around, but WipEout had a couple of extra tricks up its sleeve. One trick was the **soundtrack**, which featured popular dance music. The music appealed to an older group of gamers who were drawn to the fast action as much as they were to the pumping tunes.

The game's other trick was the special abilities found around the track. Players can pick up special boosts that give them game-changing abilities, such as rockets and mines. So you may be racing ahead of another player, but they might have a rocket, so watch out for a shot in your tail!

TECH TALK

If you're going to be a whiz at racing games, you need to know what you're talking about. This data file will zoom you through the facts about racing games and turn you into a winner. Okay, Arcade, start your engines and tell us what we need to know.

<<LOADING... DATA LEVEL THREE: WHAT YOU NEED TO KNOW>>

PLAYER INFO

You can play alone against the computer in story **mode** or against other players, either online or at home. When playing in multiplayer mode, the screen will split for each player. Start in an easy mode and then work up to the harder modes.

ADD-ONS

Add-ons can be plugged into the console or PC to add features to the game. Many racing games can be played with a regular controller. Some players like to use add-ons such as steering wheels or racing seats. You can even play racing games in **virtual reality** (VR).

VISUALS

Early games used simple **pixelated** graphics. Often the car just stayed in the center of the screen and the player controlled the track's movements to keep the car in the center. Modern games use very realistic graphics which make the player feel like they are really in the race.

CONTROLS

On a controller, there are buttons for accelerating, or going faster, and for braking, or stopping. The thumbsticks usually are used to control direction. Controllers that detect movement can be tilted and turned to steer. More advanced games will also have controls for changing **gears**.

LEVELS

Most games will offer a tutorial level to help you learn the controls. Racing games usually start off with easier tracks and slower cars, and as you complete these tracks, you unlock more difficult tracks and faster cars.

FACT FILE: PROJECT CARS 2

Each major console has its own special racing game. Nintendo has Mario Kart, PlayStation has Gran Turismo and WipEout, and Xbox has Forza. Racing fans playing on PCs, however, get the chance to play the most serious games of all, games that pride themselves on being as realistic as possible. And it's from the world of PC racing (even though it is also available on Xbox and PlayStation) that our next game comes from.

Project CARS is interesting for a number of reasons. The developer that made it, Slightly Mad Studios, invited players to contribute money, time, talent, and ideas to help create the game. This is called crowdfunding, and it's important because not only did it help the game get made, it also inspired the name. CARS stands for Community Assisted Racing Simulator.

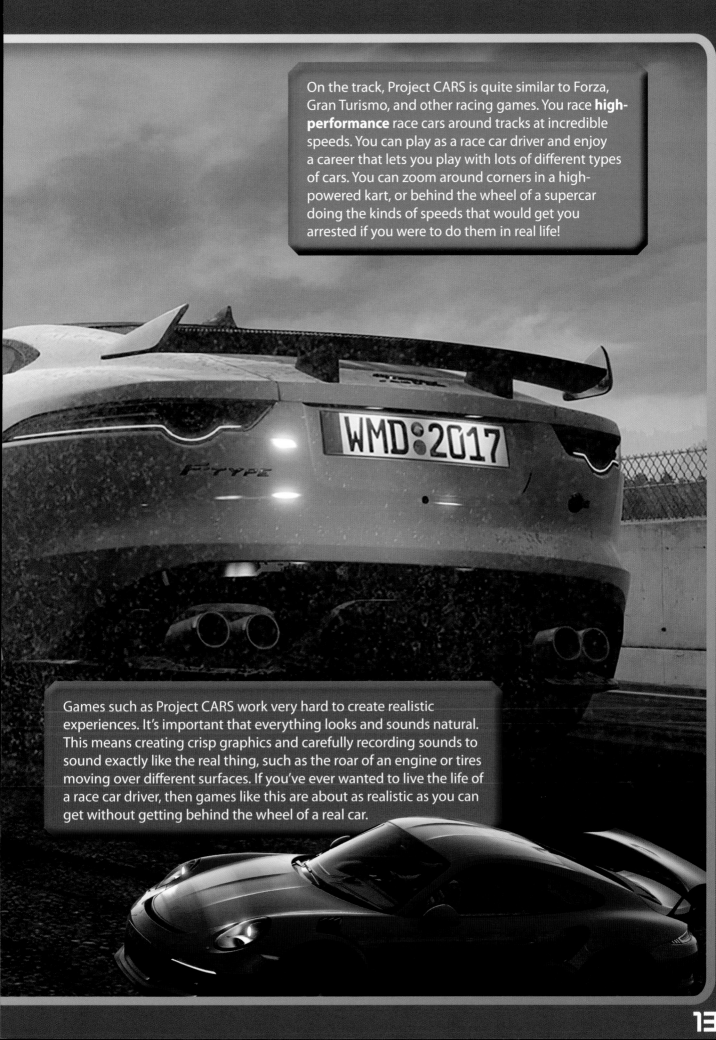

On the track, Project CARS is quite similar to Forza, Gran Turismo, and other racing games. You race **high-performance** race cars around tracks at incredible speeds. You can play as a race car driver and enjoy a career that lets you play with lots of different types of cars. You can zoom around corners in a high-powered kart, or behind the wheel of a supercar doing the kinds of speeds that would get you arrested if you were to do them in real life!

Games such as Project CARS work very hard to create realistic experiences. It's important that everything looks and sounds natural. This means creating crisp graphics and carefully recording sounds to sound exactly like the real thing, such as the roar of an engine or tires moving over different surfaces. If you've ever wanted to live the life of a race car driver, then games like this are about as realistic as you can get without getting behind the wheel of a real car.

TIMELINE OF RACING GAMES

Kick it into reverse gear—we're going back in time!
We'll need to access the archives for this one.
Okay, Arcade, please access and display timeline files.

<<LOADING... DATA LEVEL FOUR:
RACING GAMES TIMELINE>>

THE 1980s

Graphics improved, and the use of **2-D** graphics and **animations** improved the player experience. Sega's Out Run became very popular. It was one of the first games to allow the player choice over direction. The game even allowed the player to change the car's stereo!

THE 1970s

Racing arcade games became popular, including Atari's Space Race and Sega's Fonz.

EARLY 1990s

Consoles brought racing into our living rooms. 3-D graphics and more realistic games came into fashion as technology advanced. Sega led the way again with Virtua Racing, which was the first game to allow the player to choose between first-person and third-person views. Most games now use this technique.

LATE 1990s

As consoles developed, so did the games. Sony's Gran Turismo was known as the "real driving simulator" and was very realistic. It featured 140 cars and 11 tracks. Arcade-style games still proved popular, such as Sega's Crazy Taxi, one of the first **sandbox** racing games.

2000s–NOW

The 2000s saw racing games really take off. Old favorites kept getting **upgraded**, and new games such as Need For Speed: Underground (a street-racing game) and Forza Motorsport brought new ideas such as damage to cars. Racing games are getting more and more realistic.

EARLY 1960s

In 1969, Sega released the electronic game Grand Prix. It was available to be played in arcades.

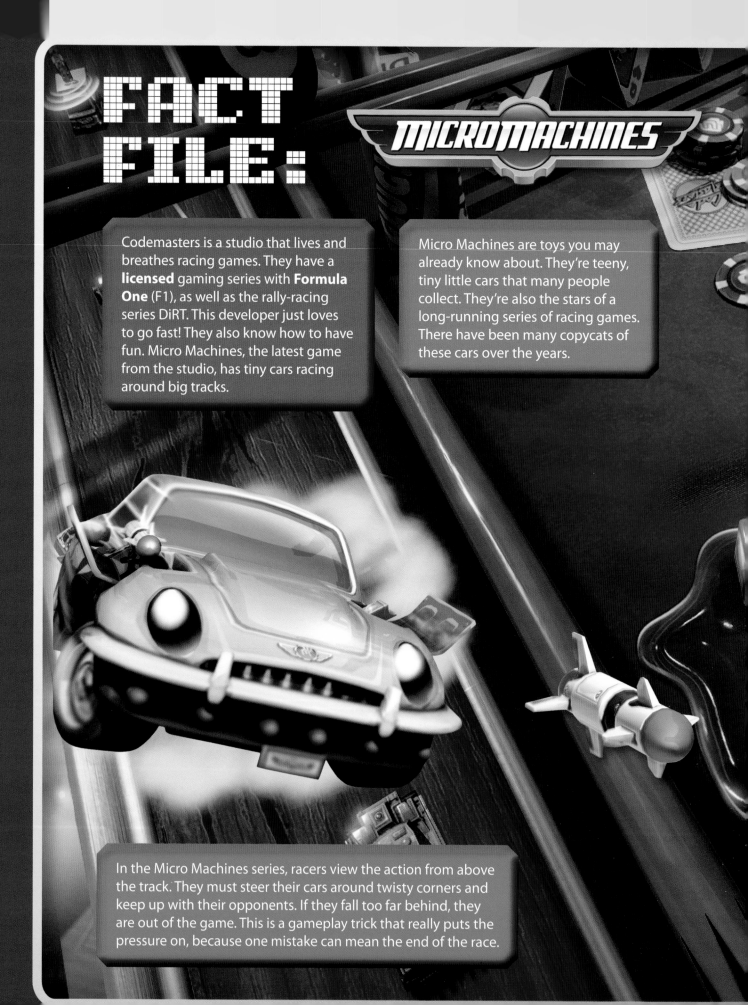

FACT FILE:

MICROMACHINES

Codemasters is a studio that lives and breathes racing games. They have a **licensed** gaming series with **Formula One** (F1), as well as the rally-racing series DiRT. This developer just loves to go fast! They also know how to have fun. Micro Machines, the latest game from the studio, has tiny cars racing around big tracks.

Micro Machines are toys you may already know about. They're teeny, tiny little cars that many people collect. They're also the stars of a long-running series of racing games. There have been many copycats of these cars over the years.

In the Micro Machines series, racers view the action from above the track. They must steer their cars around twisty corners and keep up with their opponents. If they fall too far behind, they are out of the game. This is a gameplay trick that really puts the pressure on, because one mistake can mean the end of the race.

It's probably the setting for each track that really makes these games popular. Races take place in some unusual environments. Instead of sliding your car around a real-world racetrack, these miniature cars compete inside a house, sometimes on the breakfast table!

Over the years, the series has evolved to be more than just a racing game. Today there is a battle element, where players can pick up giant hammers to smash opponents or drop mines for opponents to drive into. Sometimes the tracks even make way for battle arenas. Instead of trying to get around the **circuit** first, players have to be the one with the most points at the end of the game to win.

GET YOUR GAME ON

It's time to play! Load up your chosen racer, rev your engines, and get comfy. Okay, Arcade, please load the gaming guide.

<<LOADING... DATA LEVEL FIVE: HOW TO PLAY>>

PRESS START TO BEGIN

If you're new to racing, start with the game on an easy setting. Play the tutorial carefully to learn how to control your car. If you have played before, go right to the first race. Don't expect to win right away. Practice makes perfect!

OBJECTIVES

The aim of the game is known as your objective. In racing, you only have one—to win the race!

DECISIONS, DECISIONS

Some games let you choose your car, as well as its color, tires, and other options. Some options just look cool while others affect how the car handles. If you're new, driver **assists** are your friend. They help with steering or gears.

CONTROL FREAKS

Control is everything. Avoid constantly hitting the brake button or pushing the thumbstick too hard when steering. Make little adjustments to your direction instead. Try tapping the brakes as you go into a turn, speeding up on long straight sections, or learning how to **drift**.

GET COMPETITIVE

Racing games are all about winning. You need to carefully pass your opponents, nudging them out of the way. And if you have weapons, use them! A well-timed oil spill or shooting star might take out the competition.

<<DID YOU KNOW?>>
PRACTICE, PRACTICE, PRACTICE! THE MORE YOU PLAY AND LEARN THE PATTERNS, THE BETTER YOU WILL BE AT THE GAME.

FACT FILE: MARIOKART

The king of the family racer is definitely Mario Kart. Over the years, the little red plumber and his friends have starred in some famous games. We're going to focus on the most recent entry in the series, but it's important to remember that ever since Super Mario Kart landed on the Super Nintendo Entertainment System (SNES) back in 1992, the series has offered the very best in four-wheeled family entertainment.

4P Versus Game Available

CREDIT(S) 0/1

The latest game to land, Mario Kart 8 Deluxe, launched on Wii U and then Nintendo Switch, and it once again proved to be the perfect family racer. Thanks to assists that let even the youngest gamer compete, it's the most **accessible** racing game around. It's also one of the most colorful, with players able to tear around some tracks inspired by past games and Nintendo's worlds.

Mario Kart stars a huge number of characters from the Nintendo world. Whether you're playing as Mario, Donkey Kong, Princess Peach, or Bowser, the karts you'll be driving are exactly the same. To win, you will need the skills to take each corner perfectly, and as many power-up items as you can grab while on the track.

Power-up items include shells that you can fire at opponents, banana peels that cause people to slip all over place, and a blooper that sprays ink on other people's screens. You can even turn into a giant Bullet Bill and go extra fast and knock your opponents out of the way. When you're not on the track, you can also play various modes in more open stages, where the aim of the game isn't to finish first, but to take out as many players as you possibly can. Mario Kart's secret is that it offers a little bit of everything.

CONSOLE PROFILE

While most consoles can play all types of games, there is one company whose consoles have been linked to racing games since the very beginning: Sega. Let's find out more…

1983: THE SG-1000

Small console which took cartridges. 1–2 players. Small joystick attached.

1985: MASTER SYSTEM/SEGA MARK III

Known as Master System in Europe and the U.S., and the Sega Mark III in Japan. Upgraded to Master System II in 1990. Popular system featuring built-in titles and games on cartridges and Sega Cards. Top games included Asterix, Sonic the Hedgehog, and Alex Kidd.

1988: MEGA DRIVE/ GENESIS

16-**bit** TV console, known as Genesis in North America, or Mega Drive elsewhere. More than 900 games available, including Sonic the Hedgehog and Mortal Kombat.

1990: GAME GEAR

First handheld console for Sega.

1994: SEGA SATURN

32-bit console, played CD-ROM games. First Sega console with Internet access.

1998: SEGA DREAMCAST

Fifth and final major console for Sega. Controller featured a small screen. Discontinued in 2001.

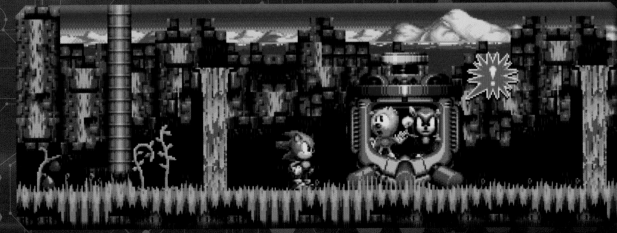

RACING LINES

As technology improves, racing simulators are becoming more lifelike. Developers work with car manufacturers to create **authentic** car models and the most realistic graphics for the games. They pay attention to even the tiniest details on the cars so that even the most knowledgeable fans will be impressed.

It's not just the cars that get a lot of attention. Game studios go to great lengths to improve the quality of the racetracks featured in games such as Forza and Gran Turismo. In the past, tracks were designed based on photographs of real tracks. Today, developers use the latest technology to map out tracks and include every detail of the real track so that players feel as if they are really driving on world-famous tracks.

It's especially important to create accurate tracks for licensed games such as the F1 series by Codemasters. Players compete in season-long campaigns against famous drivers in the latest cars. Without realistic tracks, players wouldn't feel like they were really there.

Racing games let us get behind the wheel of some iconic vehicles and race on the world's most famous circuits. Whether you like the view of racing from inside the car or a more relaxed view that puts you outside the car, you can travel the world and compete on incredibly detailed circuits, thanks to modern technology.

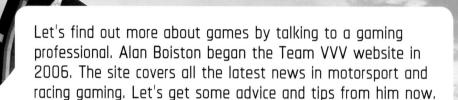

PRO TALK

Let's find out more about games by talking to a gaming professional. Alan Boiston began the Team VVV website in 2006. The site covers all the latest news in motorsport and racing gaming. Let's get some advice and tips from him now.

ALAN BOISTON

"I've been a fan of video games since the early 1980s, collecting many consoles and games while working in the U.K. games industry for over 24 years. Through retail, buying, development, TV presenting, esports, and journalism, you name it, I've probably done it. After running a successful esport team I decided to create the Team VVV website, specifically focusing on the racing gaming genre."

1. WHAT MAKES GAMES FUN TO PLAY WITH YOUR FRIENDS?

"A shared enjoyment. You all get involved and understand the skill and **mechanics** to make the most out of it. Split-screen games are best played in local multiplayer while team games tend to work well online. Both create that fun factor."

2. WHY DO WE LIKE CHALLENGING AND DIFFICULT GAMES?

"We like to test ourselves, we need a target that makes it feel like more of an achievement. When you conquer a difficult game, you feel you've been on a journey. Your gaming skills have improved, you've learned how to deal with different challenges, memorized challenging aspects, and discovered how to combat them. This delivers a sense of accomplishment that no other form of media can deliver."

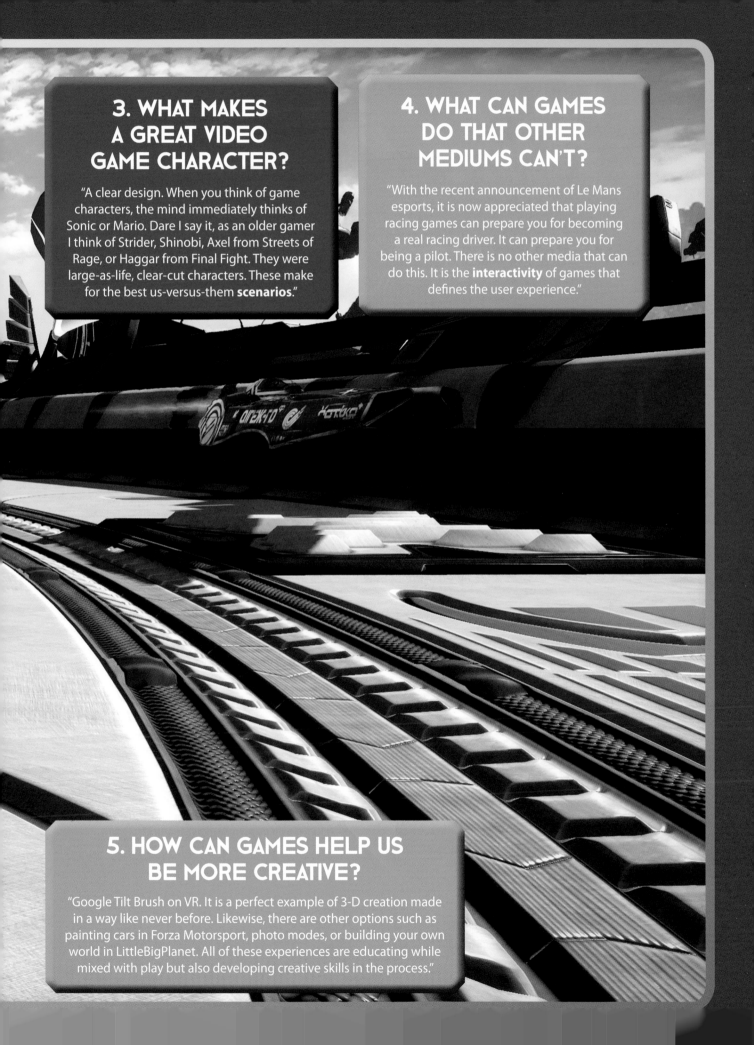

3. WHAT MAKES A GREAT VIDEO GAME CHARACTER?

"A clear design. When you think of game characters, the mind immediately thinks of Sonic or Mario. Dare I say it, as an older gamer I think of Strider, Shinobi, Axel from Streets of Rage, or Haggar from Final Fight. They were large-as-life, clear-cut characters. These make for the best us-versus-them **scenarios**."

4. WHAT CAN GAMES DO THAT OTHER MEDIUMS CAN'T?

"With the recent announcement of Le Mans esports, it is now appreciated that playing racing games can prepare you for becoming a real racing driver. It can prepare you for being a pilot. There is no other media that can do this. It is the **interactivity** of games that defines the user experience."

5. HOW CAN GAMES HELP US BE MORE CREATIVE?

"Google Tilt Brush on VR. It is a perfect example of 3-D creation made in a way like never before. Likewise, there are other options such as painting cars in Forza Motorsport, photo modes, or building your own world in LittleBigPlanet. All of these experiences are educating while mixed with play but also developing creative skills in the process."

FACT FILE:

FORZA HORIZON 4

Microsoft's **flagship** racing series comes in two flavors. One half of the series is called Forza Motorsport, while the other half is called Forza Horizon. Like Project CARS and Gran Turismo, Forza Motorsport is an arcade simulation. That means that it offers a pretty realistic experience for race fans, but there are a bunch of assists that you can turn on to make the cars a bit easier to drive. The most powerful cars can be a real challenge to control around tight corners.

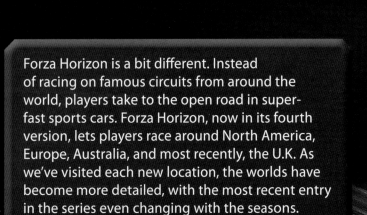

Forza Horizon is a bit different. Instead of racing on famous circuits from around the world, players take to the open road in super-fast sports cars. Forza Horizon, now in its fourth version, lets players race around North America, Europe, Australia, and most recently, the U.K. As we've visited each new location, the worlds have become more detailed, with the most recent entry in the series even changing with the seasons.

Players come across events as they explore the countryside. The better they do in these competitions, the higher their standing in the game will be. Like most other racing games, players will usually be taking on computer-controlled opponents, but more and more online features are being added to the games. In both Forza series, players race against their friends using Drivatar technology. Drivatar allows the computer to watch how you drive. It then uses that information to put a virtual version of you in your friends' games!

Games such as Forza Horizon, The Crew, and Burnout offer players huge sandbox worlds to explore. Each one is filled with more traditional racing events, gravity-defying jumps, obstacle-filled courses, and traffic to dodge on busy roads.

Learning More

The finish line! You made it, well done. We can leave the Arcade now and do a few more laps. Or, if you're not finished learning yet, you can go to these websites to find out more...

<<CONTINUE? Y/N>>
WWW.PROJECTCARSGAME.COM/

<<CONTINUE? Y/N>>
WWW.GRAN-TURISMO.COM/US/

<<CONTINUE? Y/N>>
WWW.CODEMASTERS.COM/GAME/
MICRO-MACHINES-WORLD-SERIES/

<<CONTINUE? Y/N>>
WWW.FORZAMOTORSPORT.NET/EN-US/

<<CONTINUE? Y/N>>
WWW.TEAMVVV.COM

Glossary

2-D — Short for two-dimensional, an object that has width and height

3-D — Short for three-dimensional, an object that has width, height, and length

accessible — Something which is easily used by many people

animation — Moving images, such as cartoons

assists — Settings in a racing game that either make gameplay easier or harder

authentic — The real thing, not a copy

bit — The smallest unit of information in a computer

circuit — A chosen route or track where a race will take place

console — A computer system that connects video games to a screen

drift — A driving technique where a car slides around a corner, while the driver is in control

electronic — Describes a device or machine powered by electricity

flagship — The leading one of a group

Formula One — An organization that runs an international form of auto racing

gears — The parts of an engine that control its power

graphics — Images and design on a computer screen

high-performance — Something that operates to high standards at high speeds

interactivity — The way information flows between computer and user

licensed — To have formal permission from a government or company to do something

mechanics — The working parts of something

modes — Different ways of playing a game, such as multiplayer

pixelated — An electronic image made up of small squares which can be seen

reflexes — The natural ability to react quickly

sandbox — Games where a player can wander freely, not on a set path

scenario — The setting of an event or situation

simulator — A type of game which is very realistic

soundtrack — Music that accompanies the action of a film or game

upgraded — Improved or made better

virtual reality — A three-dimensional visual world created by a computer that people can interact with while wearing a headset

<<SAVING KNOWLEDGE. DO NOT SHUT DOWN.>>

Index

<<THANKS FOR ACCESSING THE ARCADE TODAY. WE HOPE YOU HAD A PLEASANT TIME. SHUTTING DOWN IN 3... 2... 1...>>